WILDLIFE VIEWING AREAS

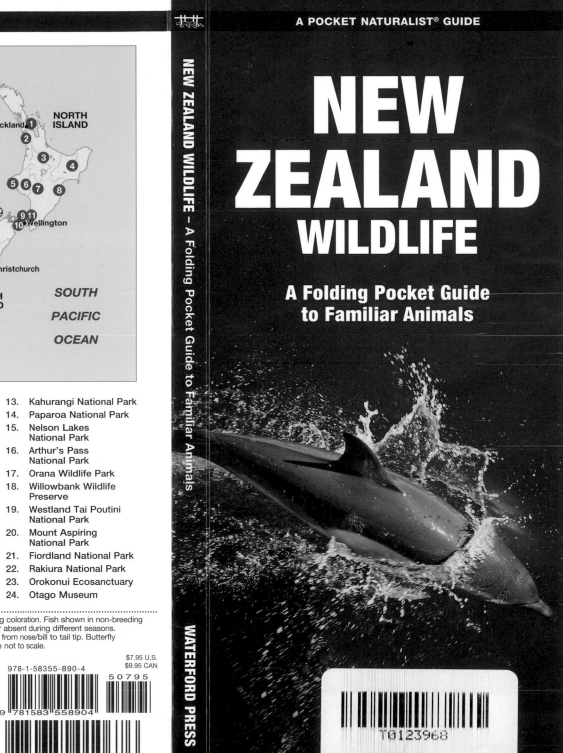

1. Auckland Zoo
2. Otorohanga Kiwi House & Native Bird Park
3. Rainbow Springs KiwiWildlife Park
4. Te Urewera National Park
5. Egmont National Park
6. Whanganui National Park
7. Tongariro National Park
8. National Aquarium of New Zealand
9. Museum of New Zealand
10. Zealandia
11. Wellington Zoo
12. Abel Tasman National Park
13. Kahurangi National Park
14. Paparoa National Park
15. Nelson Lakes National Park
16. Arthur's Pass National Park
17. Orana Wildlife Park
18. Willowbank Wildlife Preserve
19. Westland Tai Poutini National Park
20. Mount Aspiring National Park
21. Fiordland National Park
22. Rakiura National Park
23. Orokonui Ecosanctuary
24. Otago Museum

Most illustrations show the adult male in breeding coloration. In non-breeding coloration, Colors and markings may be duller or absent during different seasons. Fish shown in breeding coloration. The measurements denote the length of species from nose/bill to tail tip. Butterfly measurements denote wingspan. Illustrations are not to scale.

Waterford Press publishes reference guides that introduce readers to nature observation, outdoor recreation and survival skills. Product information is featured on the website: www.waterfordpress.com.

Text & illustrations © 2015, 2023 Waterford Press Inc. All rights reserved. Photos © Shutterstock. To order or for information on custom published products, please call 800-434-2555 or email orderdesk@waterfordpress.com. For permissions or to share comments, email editor@waterfordpress.com. 2311346

$7.95 U.S.
$9.95 CAN

978-1-58355-890-4

NEW ZEALAND WILDLIFE

A Folding Pocket Guide to Familiar Animals

INVERTEBRATES

Yellow Admiral
Bassaris itea
To 5 cm (2 in.)

Common Tussock
Argyrophenga antipodum
To 4 cm (1.5 in.)

New Zealand Red Admiral
Bassaris gonerilla
To 6 cm (2.5 in.)

Cabbage White
Pieris rapae
To 5 cm (2 in.)

Common Blue Butterfly
Zizinia atis
To 2 cm (.8 in.)

Monarch
Danaus plexippus
To 10 cm (4 in.)

Gum Emperor Moth
Opodiphthera eucalypti
To 15 cm (6 in.)

Cabbage Tree Moth
Epiphryne verriculata
To 4 cm (1.5 in.)

Woodland Ringlet
Erebia medusa
To 5 cm (2 in.)

Cinnabar Moth
Tyria jacobaeae
To 4 cm (1.5 in.)

Magpie Moth
Nyctemera annulata
To 4 cm (1.5 in.)

Huhu Beetle
Prionoplus reticularis
To 5 cm (2 in.)
The largest endemic beetle.

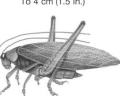

Green Katydid
Caedicia simplex
To 5 cm (2 in.)

Red Damselfly
Xanthocnemis zealandica
To 3.5 cm (1.4 in.)

New Zealand Bush Giant Dragonfly
Uropetala carovei
To 9 cm (3.5 in.)

Stick Insect
Acanthoxyla prasinus
To 15 cm (6 in.)
One of about 20 native species.

INVERTEBRATES

Giant Weta
Deinacrida heteracantha
To 9 cm (3.5 in.)
One of the world largest insects is endemic to New Zealand. Endangered.

New Zealand Mantis
Orthodera novaezealandiae
To 4 cm (1.5 in.)

Common Wasp
Vespula vulgaris
To 2 cm (.8 in.)
Can sting repeatedly.

Paper Wasp
Polistes chinensis
To 2.5 cm (.9 in.)
Builds papery nests. Can sting repeatedly.

Giant Ichneumon Wasp
Rhyssa persuasoria
To 4 cm (1.5 in.)

Bumblebee
Bombus spp.
To 2.5 cm (.9 in.)
Four species of this furry bee were introduced in 1885 to improve plant pollination.

Honey Bee
Apis mellifera
To 2 cm (.8 in.)
Slender bee has pollen baskets on its rear legs. Can only sting once.

Helm's Stag Beetle
Geodorcus helmsi
To 4 cm (1.5 in.)
One of about 25 similar species found in New Zealand.

Crane Fly
Austrotipula hudsoni
To 4 cm (1.5 in.)
One of about 500 similar species found in New Zealand.

Plaster Bee
Leioproctus spp.
To 1 cm (.4 in.)

Backswimmer
Family Notonectidae
To 1.3 cm (.5 in.)
Swims on its back and often rests at or just below the surface.

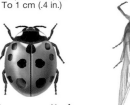

Eleven-spotted Ladybird
Coccinella undecimpunctata
To 1 cm (.4 in.)
One of over 30 similar species.

Clapping Cicada
Amphipsalta spp.
To 3 cm (1 in.)
Summer choruses of males "clapping" can be deafening.

Water Boatman
Family Corixidae
To .8 cm (.3 in.)
Uses flattened limbs to "row" in quiet, clear waters.

SPIDERS

Wolf Spider
Lycosa hilaris
To 2 cm (.8 in.)
Does not weave webs but catches prey by chasing it down and pouncing on it.

Nurseryweb Spider
Dolomedes minor
To 2 cm (.8 in.)
Builds web shelter for its young which it guards until they become independent. A fishing spider, it is found on the edges of small pools.

Katipo Spider
Latrodectus katipo
To 1 cm (.4 in.)
Pea-sized, venomous spider has a glossy black abdomen with a red stripe down the middle.

White-tailed Spider
Lampona cylindrata
To 2 cm (.8 in.)
Aggressive and venomous.

Trapdoor Spider
Stanwella grisea
To 5 cm (2 in.)
Lives in a silk-lined burrow camouflaged by a hinged flap (trapdoor). When prey walks by, it flips open the flap and pounces on it.

FISHES

Koaro
Galaxias brevipinnis To 18 cm (7 in.)

Inanga
Galaxias maculatus To 20 cm (8 in.)

Bully
Gobiomorphus spp. To 20 cm (8 in.)

Giant Kokopu
Galaxias argenteus To 60 cm (2 ft.)

Perch
Perca fluviatilis To 60 cm (2 ft.)

Longfin Eel
Anguilla dieffenbachii
To 2 m (6.5 ft.)
Note large size.

Quinnat Salmon
Oncorhynchus tshawytscha
To 1.5 m (5 ft.)
Has dark spots on back and tail. The world's largest salmon was introduced in the late 1800s.

FISHES

Brown Trout
Salmo trutta To 1 m (40 in.)
Has red and black spots on its body.

Rainbow Trout
Oncorhynchus mykiss
To 1.1 m (44 in.)
Note reddish side stripe.

Brook Trout
Salvelinus fontinalis To 70 cm (28 in.)
Reddish side spots have blue halos.

Tench
Tinca tinca To 70 cm (28 in.)

REPTILES & AMPHIBIANS

Tuatara
Sphenodon punctatus
To 25 cm (10 in.)
Unique, prehistoric-looking reptile has no external ears and three eyes. Endemic to New Zealand, it has no living relatives.

Common Gecko
Hoplodactylus maculatus
To 15 cm (6 in.)
The most common and widespread gecko in NZ.

Jeweled Geckos
Naultinus spp.
To 20 cm (8 in.)
Widespread genus of green geckos is composed of nine species found throughout NZ.

Forest Gecko
Hoplodactylus granulatus
To 20 cm (8 in.)
Chameleon-like, it is able to adjust its coloration to match its environment.

Common Skink
Oligosoma nigriplantare
To 15 cm (6 in.)

Copper Skink
Cyclodina aenea
To 10 cm (4 in.)

Whistling Frog
Litoria ewingi
To 5 cm (2 in.)
Call is a whistled – *weep-weep-weep.*

Green Bell-frog
Litoria aurea
To 10 cm (4 in.)

Growling Grass Frog
Litoria raniformis
To 10 cm (4 in.)
Low moaning call has been compared to the sound of a duck being strangled.

BIRDS

Brown Kiwi
Apteryx australis
To 40 cm (16 in.)

Great Crested Grebe
Podiceps cristatus
To 50 cm (20 in.)

Feral Goose
Anser anser
To 83 cm (33 in.)
Note thick neck.

Black Swan
Cygnus atratus
To 1.4 m (56 in.)

Canada Goose
Branta canadensis
To 1.1 m (45 in.)

Australasian Shoveler
Anas rhynchotis
To 55 cm (22 in.)
Large bill is wedge-shaped.

Blue Penguin
Eudyptula minor
To 40 cm (16 in.)
Also known as fairy penguin and little penguin.

Mallard
Anas platyrhynchos
To 70 cm. (28 in.)

Little Shag
Phalacrocorax melanoleucos
To 60 cm (2 ft.)

Royal Spoonbill
Platalea regia
To 75 cm (30 in.)
Bill has a spoon-shaped tip.

Paradise Shelduck
Tadorna variegata
To 65 cm (26 in.)

White-faced Heron
Ardea novaehollandiae
To 65 cm (26 in.)

Pied Stilt
Himantopus leucocephalus
To 40 cm (16 in.)

Reef Heron
Egretta sacra
To 65 cm (26 in.)

BIRDS

Eastern Rosella
Platycercus eximius
To 33 cm (13 in.)

Kaka
Nestor meridionalis
To 45 cm (18 in.)

Kea
Nestor notabilis
To 45 cm (18 in.)
The world's only alpine parrot.

Black-billed Gull
Larus bulleri
To 38 cm (19 in.)

Southern Black-backed Gull
Larus dominicanus
To 58 cm (23 in.)
Note all-white tail.

Yellow-crowned Parakeet
Cyanoramphus auriceps
To 25 cm (10 in.)

Australasian Harrier
Circus approximans
To 60 cm (2 ft.)

Morepork
Ninox novaeseelandiae
To 35 cm (14 in.)
Name-saying call – more-pork – is a common nighttime sound.

Song Thrush
Turdus philomelos
To 23 cm (9 in.)
Named for its rich, loud, clear song which is a series of repeated phrases separated by brief pauses.

Tui
Prosthemadera novaeseelandiae
To 30 cm (12 in.)

Bellbird
Anthornis melanura
To 20 cm (8 in.)

Skylark
Alauda arvensis
To 18 cm (7 in.)

Rifleman
Acanthisitta chloris
To 8 cm (3 in.)

New Zealand Fantail
Rhipidura spp.
To 15 cm (6 in.)

BIRDS

New Zealand Pigeon
Hemiphaga novaeseelandiae
To 50 cm (20 in.)

Silvereye
Zosterops lateralis
To 13 cm (5 in.)
Note prominent white eye ring.

Rock Dove
Columba livia
To 35 cm (14 in.)

New Zealand Kingfisher
Halcyon sancta vagans
To 25 cm (10 in.)

Tomtit
Petroica macrocephala
To 13 cm (5 in.)

Shining Cuckoo
Chrysococcyx lucidus
To 20 cm (8 in.)
Green plumage is metallic.

Welcome Swallow
Hirundo neoxena
To 15 cm (6 in.)

Gray Warbler
Gerygone igata
To 10 cm (4 in.)

Long-tailed Cuckoo
Eudynamys taitensis
To 40 cm (16 in.)

Starling
Sturnus vulgaris
To 20 cm (8 in.)

Myna
Acridotheres tristis
To 23 cm (9 in.)

Blackbird
Turdus merula
To 25 cm (10 in.)
Females are brownish.

Australian Magpie
Gymnorhina tibicen
To 40 cm (16 in.)

Masked Lapwing
Vanellus miles
To 38 cm (15 in.)
Also called spur-winged plover.

New Zealand Pipit
Anthus novaeseelandiae
To 20 cm (8 in.)
Constantly flicks its tail while foraging.

BIRDS

Yellowhammer
Emberiza citrinella
To 15 cm (6 in.)

Greenfinch
Chloris chloris
To 15 cm (6 in.)
Female is similar but paler green.

Chaffinch
Fringilla coelebs
To 15 cm (6 in.)

Goldfinch
Carduelis carduelis
To 13 cm (5 in.)

Redpoll
Acanthis flammea
To 13 cm (5 in.)

House Sparrow
Passer domesticus
To 15 cm (6 in.)

MAMMALS

Hedgehog
Erinaceus europaeus
To 30 cm (12 in.)
Introduced from Europe in the 1870s to help control garden pests.

New Zealand Long-tailed Bat
Chalinolobus tuberculatus
To 8 cm (3 in.)
Endemic species.

House Mouse
Mus musculus
To 20 cm (8 in.)
Introduced pest has a naked tail.

Kiore
Rattus exulans
To 30 cm (12 in.)
The smallest rat in New Zealand.

Hare
Lepus capensis
To 60 cm (2 ft.)
Introduced in 1851.

Ship Rat
Rattus rattus
To 45 cm (18 in.)
Black rodent has a naked tail. Also called black rat.

Rabbit
Oryctolagus cuniculus
To 60 cm (2 ft.)
Introduced in 1777 as a source of meat.

Norway Rat
Rattus norvegicus
To 45 cm (18 in.)
Brown to gray rodent has a naked tail.

MAMMALS

Brushtail Possum
Trichosurus vulpecula
To 80 cm (32 in.)
Introduced in the 1850s to establish a fur industry.

Weasel
Mustela nivalis
To 20 cm (8 in.)
Introduced from Europe in the 1870s.

Ferret
Mustela furo
To 60 cm (2 ft.)
Introduced from Europe in the 1870s to help control the rabbit plague.

Stoat
Mustela erminea To 35 cm (14 in.)
Note white feet. Coat may turn white in winter in the coldest regions. Also called ermine.

Tahr
Hemitragus jemlahicus
To 1.4 m (56 in.)
Himalayan mountain goat was introduced to the Southern Alps in 1904.

Feral Goat
Capra hircus
To 1.5 m (5 ft.)
Introduced from Europe in 1770s.

Red-necked Wallaby
Macropus rufogriseus
To 1.6 m (5.3 ft.)
Note red nape.

Wild Boar
Sus scrofa To 1.8 m (6 ft.)
Introduced from Europe in 1769.

Chamois
Rupicapra rupicapra
To 1.5 m (5 ft.)
Introduced from Europe in 1907.

Fallow Deer
Dama dama
To 1.7 m (5.5 ft.)
Coat color varies from white to dark chestnut but most are brownish in the summer and sooty in winter.

Red Deer
Cervus elaphus To 2.7 m (8.8 ft.)
The most abundant deer.

Feral Horse
Equus caballus To 2.1 m (7 ft.)
Wild herds are found in the Kaimanawa Range and Aupouri Peninsula.

MARINE MAMMALS

Leopard Seal *Hydrurga leptonyx* To 3.6 m (12 ft.)
Top predator feeds on fish, penguins and other seals.

New Zealand Fur Seal
Arctocephalus forsteri
To 3 m (10 ft.)

Southern Elephant Seal
Mirounga leonina To 6 m (20 ft.)
Has a huge over-hanging snout.

New Zealand Sea Lion
Phocarctos hookeri
To 3 m (10 ft.)

Orca
Orcinus orca
To 9 m (30 ft.)
Not a true whale, it is related to dolphins.

Common Dolphin
Delphinus delphis To 2.7 m (9 ft.)

Striped Dolphin
Stenella coeruleoalba To 2.7 m (9 ft.)

Bottlenosed Dolphin
Tursiops truncatus To 3.6 m (12 ft.)

Hector's Dolphin
Cephalorhynchus hectori
To 1.5 m (5 ft.)
The world's smallest dolphin is endemic to New Zealand.

Long-finned Pilot Whale
Globicephala melas To 6 m (20 ft.)

Sperm Whale
Physeter macrocephalus
To 21 m (70 ft.)